On the Bhagavad-Gita

By T. Subba Row
C. Jinarajadasa

Copyright © 2021 Lamp of Trismegistus. All rights reserved. No part of this publication may be reproduced or transmitted in any form or by any means, electronic or mechanical, including photocopying, recording, or by any information storage and retrieval system, without permission in writing from Lamp of Trismegistus. Reviewers may quote brief passages.

ISBN: 978-1-63118-575-5

*Esoteric Classics:
Eastern Studies*

Other Books in this Series and Related Titles

Aurora of the Philosophers by Paracelsus (978-1-63118-507-6)

Clairvoyance and Psychic Abilities by A Besant &c (978-1-63118-403-1)

The Feminine Occult by various authors (978-1-63118-711-7)

Rosicrucian Rules, Secret Signs, Codes and Symbols by various (978-1-63118-488-8)

An Outline of Theosophy by C W Leadbeater (978-1-63118-452-9)

Paracelsus, the Four Elements and Their Spirits by M P Hall (978-1-63118-400-0)

Essays on Ancient Magic by Helena P Blavatsky (978-1-63118-535-9)

Essays on the Esoteric Tradition of Karma by A Besant &c (978-1-63118-426-0)

The Use of Evil by Annie Besant (978-1-63118-532-8)

The Alchemical Catechism of Paracelsus by Paracelsus (978-1-63118-513-7)

Alchemy in the Nineteenth Century by Helena P Blavatsky (978-1-63118-446-8)

Qabbalistic Teachings and the Tree of Life by M P Hall (978-1-63118-482-6)

The Historic, Mythic and Mystic Christ by Annie Besant (978–1–63118–533–5)

The Hidden Mysteries of Christianity by Annie Besant (978–1–63118–534–2)

History, Analysis and Secret Tradition of the Tarot by Hall &c (978-1-63118-445-1)

Crystal Vision Through Crystal Gazing by Frater Achad (978-1-63118-455-0)

The Golden Verses of Pythagoras: Five Translations (978-1-63118-479-6)

Arcane Formulas or Mental Alchemy by W W Atkinson (978-1-63118-459-8)

The Machinery of the Mind by Dion Fortune (978-1-63118-451-2)

The A E Waite Reader: A Selection of Occult Essays (978-1-63118-515-1)

The Leadbeater Reader: A Selection of Occult Essays (978-1-63118-483-3)

Audio versions are also available on Audible, Amazon and Apple

Other Books in this Series and Related Titles

What Theosophy Does for Us by C W Leadbeater (978–1–63118–574–8)

Spiritual Life for Man by Annie Besant (978–1–63118–573–1)

The Mysteries by Annie Besant (978–1–63118–572–4)

Fundamental Ideas of Theosophy by Bhagwan Das (978–1–63118–571–7)

Dreams: What They Are and Caused by C W Leadbeater (978–1–63118–570–0)

Communication Between Different Worlds by Annie Besant (978–1–63118–569–4)

Animism, Magic and the Omnipotence of Thought by S Freud (978–1–63118–568–7)

Buddhism by F Otto Schrader (978–1–63118–567–0)

Death by W W Westcott (978–1–63118–566–3)

The Religion of Theosophy by Bhagwan Das (978–1–63118–565–6)

The Spirit of Zoroastrianism by Henry S Olcott (978–1–63118–564–9)

The Brotherhood of Religions by Annie Besant (978–1–63118–563–2)

Fourth Book of Maccabees by Josephus (978-1-63118-562-5)

The Story of Ahikar by Ahiqar (978-1-63118-561-8)

Vision of the Spirit by C. Jinarajadasa (978-1-63118-560-1)

Occult Arts by William Q. Judge (978-1-63118-559-5)

Kali the Mother by Sister Nivedita (978-1-63118-558-8)

Love and Death by Sri Aurobindo (978–1–63118–557–1)

Times and Seasons Volume 1, Numbers 4-6 (978-1-63118-556-4)

Interesting Account of Several Remarkable Visions (978-1-63118-553-3)

Private Diary of Joseph Smith 1832-1834 (978-1-63118-546-5)

Audio versions are also available on Audible, Amazon and Apple

Table of Contents

Introduction...7

On the Bhagavad-Gita
By T. Subba Row & Nobin K. Bannerji...9

On the Bhagavad-Gita
By T. Babu Saheb Nobin K. Bannerji...17

The Bhagavad-Gita
By C. Jinarajadasa...27

INTRODUCTION

The word "esoteric" can be difficult to define. Esotericism in general can be seen less as a system of beliefs and more as a category, which encompasses numerous, different systems of beliefs. It's a bit of juxtaposition, since the word "esoteric" indicates something that few people know about, while the term itself broadly covers numerous philosophies, practices, areas of study and belief systems.

In a greater sense, Esotericism acts as a storehouse for secret knowledge, which is often considered ancient (by *tradition, if not by fact),* passed down from generation to generation, in private. At various times in history, simply possessing the knowledge of some of these subjects, was considered illegal and a jailable offence, if discovered. This usually included such general topics as Alchemy, Pharmacology, Qabalah, Hermeticism, Occultism, Ceremonial Magic, Astrology, Divination, Rosicrucianism and so on. Collectively, these areas of study were often referred to as the esoteric sciences.

Sometimes, the outer garment of a subject isn't esoteric, while what is hidden beneath it, is. As an example, Freemasonry isn't necessarily esoteric by nature (at *least not anymore),* but certain signs, passwords and handshakes given to the candidate during their initiation, are in fact, esoteric, in the sense that they are hidden from the general public.

Today, in the twenty-first century, such topics are readily available at bookstores across the country, and numerous mainsteam publishers offer beginners guides and coffee-table volumes on many of these subjects, intended for mass appeal. Books like *"The Secret"* have turned previously arcane topics into household knowledge. All that being the case, however, it isn't to say that there still aren't buried secrets to uncover, ancient wisdom being ignored and forgotten mysteries to be explored. In fact, it is often that we are only able to further our own studies by standing on the shoulders of these disappearing giants.

Lamp of Trismegistus is doing its part to help preserve humanity's esoteric history by making some of these classics available to those students who are seeking to unearth the knowledge of these ancient colossi.

So, be sure to check other titles from our *Esoteric Classics* series, as well as our *Occult Fiction, Theosophical Classics, Foundations of Freemasonry Series, Supernatural Fiction, Paranormal Research Series, Studies in Buddhism* and our *Christian Apocrypha Series.* You can also download the audio versions of most of these titles from Amazon, Apple or Audible, for learning on the go.

ON THE BHAGAVAD-GITA

by T. Subba Row and Nobin K. Bannerji

In studying the *Bhagavad-Gîtâ* it must not be treated as if isolated from the rest of the *Mahâbhârata* as it at present exists. It was inserted by Vyâsa in the right place with special reference to some of the incidents in that book. One must first realize the real position of Arjuna and Krshna in order to appreciate, the teaching of the latter. Among other appellations, Arjuna has one very strange name - he is called at different times by ten or eleven names, most of which are explained by himself in Virâtaparva. One name is omitted from the list, *viz.*, Nara. This word simply means ' man'. But why a particular man should be called by this as a proper name may at first sight appear strange. Nevertheless herein lies a clue which enables us to understand, not only the position of the *Bhagavad-Gîtâ* in the text, and its connection with Arjuna and Krshna, but the entire current running through the whole of the *Mahâbhârata,* implying Vyâsa's real views on the origin, trials and destiny of man. Vyâsa looked upon Arjuna as man, or rather the real monad in man; and upon Krshna as the Logos, or the Spirit that comes to save man. To some it appears strange that this highly philosophical teaching should have been inserted in a place apparently utterly unfitted for it. The discourse is alleged to have taken place between Arjuna and Krshna just before the battle began to rage. But when once you begin to appreciate the *Mahâbhârata,* you will see this was the fittest place for the *Bhagavad-Gîtâ.*

Historically the great battle was a struggle between two families. Philosophically it is the great battle in which the human Spirit has to fight against the lower passions in the physical body. Many of our readers have probably heard about the so-called '*Dweller on the*

Threshold,' so vividly described in Lytton's novel, *Zanoni*. According to this author's description, the Dweller on the Threshold seems to be some elemental, or other monster of mysterious form, appearing before the neophyte just as he is about to enter the mysterious land, and attempting to shake his resolution with menaces of unknown dangers if he is not fully prepared.

There is no such monster in reality. The description must be taken in a figurative sense. But nevertheless there is a Dweller on the Threshold, whose influence on the mental plane is far more trying than any physical terror can be. The real Dweller on the Threshold is formed of the despair and despondency of the neophyte, who is called upon to give up all his old affections for kindred, parents and children, as well as his aspirations for objects of worldly ambition, which have perhaps been his associates for many incarnations. When called upon to give up these things, the neophyte feels a kind of blank, before he realizes his higher possibilities. After having given up all his associations, his life itself seems to vanish into thin air. He seems to have lost all hope, and to have no object to live and work for. He sees no signs of his own future progress. All before him seems darkness; and a sort of pressure comes upon the soul, under which it begins to droop, and in most cases he begins to fall back and gives up further progress. But in the case of a man who really struggles, he will battle against that despair, and be able to proceed on the Path. I may here refer you to a few passages in Mill's autobiography. Of course the author knew nothing of Occultism; but there was one stage in his mental life, which seems to have come on at a particular point of his career and to have closely resembled what I have been describing. Mill was a great analytical philosopher. He made an exhaustive analysis of all mental processes,— mind, emotions, and will.

I now saw, or thought I saw, what I had always before received with incredulity - that the habit of analysis has a tendency to wear away the feelings, as indeed it has when no other mental habit is cultivated. * * * Thus neither selfish nor unselfish pleasures were pleasures to me.

At last he came to have analyzed the whole man into nothing. At this point a kind of melancholy came over him, which had something of terror in it. In this state of mind he continued for some years, until he read a copy of Wordsworth's poems full of sympathy for natural objects and human life. "From them," he says, "I seemed to learn what would be the perennial sources of happiness, when all the greater evils of life should have been removed." This feebly indicates what the chela must experience when he has determined to renounce all old associates, and is called to live for a bright future on a higher plane. This transition stage was more or less the position of Arjuna before the discourse in question. He was about to engage in a war of extermination against foes led by some of his nearest relations, and he not unnaturally shrank from the thought of killing kindred and friends. We are each of us called upon to kill out all our passions and desires, not that they are all necessarily evil in themselves, but that their influence must be annihilated before we can establish ourselves on the higher planes. The position of Arjuna is intended to typify that of a chela, who is called upon to face the Dweller on the Threshold. As the guru prepares his chela for the trials of Initiation by philosophical teaching, so at this critical point Krshna proceeds to instruct Arjuna.

The *Bhagavad-Gîtâ* may be looked upon as a discourse addressed by a guru to a chela who has fully determined upon the renunciation of all worldly desires and aspirations but yet feels a certain despondency, caused by the apparent blankness of his existence.

The book contains eighteen chapters all intimately connected. Each chapter describes a particular phase or aspect of human life. The student should bear this in mind in reading the book, and endeavour to work out the correspondences. He will find what appear to be unnecessary repetitions. These were a necessity of the method adopted by Vyâsa, his intention being to represent nature in different ways, as seen from the standpoints of the various philosophical schools which flourished in India.

As regards the moral teaching of the *Bhagavad-Gîtâ*, it is often asserted by those who do not appreciate the benefits of occult study, that, if everybody pursued this course, the world would come to a standstill; and, therefore, that this teaching can only be useful to the few, and not to ordinary people. This is not so. It is of course true that the majority of men are not in the position to give up their duties as citizens and members of families. But Krshna distinctly states that these duties, if not reconcilable with ascetic life in a forest, can certainly be reconciled with that kind of mental abnegation which is far more powerful in the production of effects on the higher planes than any physical separation from the world. For though the ascetic's body may be in the jungle, his thoughts may be in the world. Krshna therefore teaches that the real importance lies not in physical but in mental isolation. Every man who has duties to discharge must devote his mind to them. But, says the teacher, it is one thing to perform an action as a matter of duty, and another thing to perform the same from inclination, interest, or desire. It is thus plain that it is in the power of a man to make definite progress in the development of his higher faculties, whilst there is nothing noticeable in his mode of life to distinguish him from his fellows. No religion teaches that men should be the slaves of interest and desire. Few inculcate the necessity of seclusion and asceticism. The great objection that has been brought against Hinduîsm and

Buddhism is that by recommending such a mode of life to students of Occultism they tend to render void the lives of men engaged in ordinary avocations. This objection however rests upon a misapprehension. For those religions teach that it is not the nature of the act, but the mental attitude of its performer, that is of importance. This is the moral teaching that runs through the whole of the *Bhagavad-Gîtâ*. The reader should note carefully the various arguments by which Krshna establishes his proposition. He will find an account of the origin and destiny of the human monad, and of the manner in which it attains salvation through the aid and enlightenment derived from its Logos. Some have taken Krshna's exhortation to Arjuna to worship him alone as supporting the doctrine of a personal God. But this is an erroneous conclusion. For, though speaking of himself as Parabrahm, Krshna is still the Logos. He describes himself as Âtma, but no doubt is *one* with Parabrahm, as there is no essential difference between Âtma and Parabrahm. Certainly the Logos can speak of itself as Parabrahm. So all sons of God, including Christ, have spoken of themselves as one with the Father. His saying that He exists in almost every entity in the Cosmos expresses strictly an attribute of Parabrahm. But a Logos, being a manifestation of Parabrahm, can use these words and assume these attributes. Thus Krshna only calls upon Arjuna to worship his own highest Spirit, through which alone he can hope to attain salvation. Krshna is teaching Arjuna what the Logos in the course of Initiation will teach the human monad, pointing out that through himself alone is salvation to be obtained. This implies no idea of a personal God.

Again, notice the view of Krshna respecting the Sânkhya philosophy. Some strange ideas are afloat about this system. It is supposed that the Sûtras we possess represent the original aphorisms of Kapila. But this has been denied by many great teachers, including Shankarâchârya, who says that they do not represent his real views, but those of some other Kapila, or the writer of the book. The real Sânkhya philosophy is identical with the Pythagorean system of numerals, and the philosophy embodied in the Chaldæn system of numbers. The philosopher's object was to represent all the mysterious powers of nature by a few simple formulæ, which he expressed in numerals. The original book is not to be found, though it is possible that it still exists. The system now put forward under this name contains little beyond an account of the evolution of the elements and a few combinations of the same which enter into the formation of the various tatwams. Krshna reconciles the Sânkhya philosophy, Râja Yoga, and even Hatha Yoga, by first pointing out that the philosophy, if properly understood, leads to the same merging of the human monad in the Logos. The doctrine of karma, which embraces a wider field than that allowed it by orthodox pandits, who have limited its signification solely to religious observances, is the same in all philosophies, and is made by Krshna to include almost every good and bad act or even thought. The student must first go through the *Bhagavad-Gîtâ*, and next try to differentiate the teachings in the eighteen different parts under different categories. He should observe how these different aspects branch out from one common centre, and how the teachings in these chapters are intended to do away with the objections of different philosophers, to the occult theory and the path of salvation here pointed out. If this is done, the book will show the real attitude of Occultists in considering the nature of the Logos and the human monad. In this way almost all that is held sacred in different systems is combined. By such teaching Krshna succeeds in dispelling Arjuna's despondency and in giving him a higher idea of the nature of the force acting through him, though for the time being it is manifesting itself as a distinct individual. He overcomes Arjuna's disinclination to fight, by analyzing the idea of self, and showing that the man is in error, who thinks that *he* is doing this, that or the other. When it is found that what he calls 'I' is a sort of fiction, created by his own ignorance, a great part of the difficulty has ceased to exist. He further proceeds to demonstrate the existence of a higher individuality, of which Arjuna had no previous knowledge. Then he points out that this individuality is connected with the Logos. He furthermore expounds the nature of the Logos and shows that it is Parabrahm. This is the substance of the first eleven or twelve chapters. In those that follow, Krshna gives Arjuna further teaching in order to make him firm of purpose; and explains to him how, through the inherent qualities of Prakrti and Pûrusha, all the entities have been brought into existence.

It is to be observed that the number eighteen is constantly recurring in the *Mahâbhârata,* seeing that it contains eighteen Parvâs, the contending armies were divided into eighteen army corps, the battle raged eighteen days, and the book is called by a name which means eighteen. This number is mysteriously connected with Arjuna. I have been describing him as man, but even Parabrahm manifests itself as a Logos in more ways than one. Krshna may be the Logos, but only one particular form of it. The number eighteen is to represent this particular form. Krshna is the Logos that overshadows the human Ego and his gift of his sister in marriage to Arjuna typifies the union between the light of the Logos and the human monad. It is worthy of note that Arjuna did not want Krshna to fight for him, but only to act as his charioteer and to be his friend and counsellor. From this it will be perceived that the human soul must fight its own battle, assisted, when once the human being begins to tread the true Path, by his own Logos.

ON THE BHAGAVAD-GITA

by Babu Saheb Nobin K. Bannerji

The portion of the great epic poem, the *Mahâbhârata*, known as the *Bhagavad-Gîtâ* is considered by all as the noblest record left in India by the venerable sage, the holy Vyâsa, also called Shri Veda Vyâsa, or Bâdarâyana. It is held in the highest esteem by both the Hindus and the Buddhists, and the instinctive veneration paid to it is great, though portions of it are directly opposed to the Vedâs. So great, indeed, is the respect that while almost every other book of the Hindu scriptures has been disfigured more or less by the interpolations made by various erudite ignoramuses - Pandits and Brâhmanas - and even the rest of the *Mahâbhârata*, in which it is incorporated, is so mutilated by later additions that, even in the number of verses and its division into chapters, no two manuscripts can be had in India which would tally with each other - no one has, unto this day, added to or taken away from the main text of the *Bhagavad-Gîtâ* one single sentence, a word, a letter, or even a comma.

The word 'Hinduism' has now become so pregnant with various meanings that, to a foreigner, it is almost an incomprehensible term. We are all Hindus, yet our sects are many and at utter variance with each other. There are the Shaivas, the Souras, and the Gânâpattyas - all, not only at wide variance with, but bitterly opposed to each other, and always at loggerheads.

There are the Vedântins, who include pantheists, deists, and the chârvâkas, atheists and materialists; and yet all of them are Hindus. In short, every system of religion and philosophy, provided it does not countenance beef-eating, may come under that name. Exoteric Hinduism consists at the present time - so far as the numerous sects of theists agree with one another - in a common and profound veneration for the Vedas, the *Bhagavad-Gîtâ*, the Pranava, (*i.e.,* Aum), the Gâyatrî, the Ganga—(Ganges *alias* Bhâgirathee)—and Gaya. In *esoteric* Hinduism, the scriptures of every sect agree in recommending to their votaries, initiation into and the practice of Râja Yoga under competent Gurus, as the only means of attaining knowledge, and, through it, Mukti or Nirvâna. Furthermore being unanimous on those points, they all teach that there is no means of emancipation; or release from the sorrows of life; and that every man must enjoy or suffer as the case may be, the consequences of his karma, or the result of his combined actions (including thoughts), and that the latter is inevitable.

In the *Bhagavad-Gîtâ*, Krshna is made to say to Arjuna that He incarnates on this earth, from time to time, for the purpose of restoring the true religion:

Whenever there is a relaxation of duty, in the world, O son of Bharata! and an increase of impiety, I then manifest (incarnate) myself for the protection of the good and the destruction of the evil-doers.

Nowhere do we find Him speaking to the contrary: and yet the Pouraniks - finding that the teaching of Gautama Buddha, inculcating a religion of pure morality, threatened their pockets - spread the idea that the missions of the ninth Avatâra was to vitiate and corrupt pure Hinduism, and substitute in its stead, atheism! It is in this connection that I have a few questions to ask of my Hindû-pandit-brothers.

(1) Who is it who says that, in the ninth Incarnation, Buddha has inculcated a false religion?

(2) When was it said - before or after the declaration of Krshna in the *Bhagavat-Gîtâ*, as quoted above?

(3) Is he, who said so, a higher and more reliable authority than Krshna was?

(4) Kapila is referred to in the *Bhagavad-Gîtâ* as also an Avatâra, although not as high as one of the ten principal Incarnations, one of whom was Buddha. In his *Sânkhya Darshana*, Kapila declares clearly his Îshwarasiddi, *i.e.,* the disapproval of Îshwara, or of the so-called God.

(5) Brhaspati - the most learned of the learned and the 'Priest of the Gods,' in his Chârvâk system of philosophy, clearly set down that there is no such thing as what is popularly called God; and he goes so far as even to deny a hereafter and teach the same.

If then Sânkhya is regarded in the light of a high authority, and Chârvâk is tolerated, why should then Buddha Darsana be cried down? Is it only because the former two, while both denying the existence of a God, and a life hereafter, do not step as hard as Buddhism does upon the corns of the priestcraft by enforcing a most sublime and uncompromising morality?

Now, the fact appears to me simply this: the work of religious reform, begun by Krshna, was completed by Buddha. Any one, who will read the *Bhagavad-Gîtâ*, and compare it with the Buddhist *Tripitaka*, will easily find this out. Hence the value placed on the *Bhagavad- Gîtâ* by the Buddhists; and the reason why they have so much less deviated from their primitive faith than we - the Hindus.

There are still Orientalists who hold to the opinion that the *Mahâbhârata* is anterior to the *Râmâyana,* for the reason that, while the latter dwells on monogamy, the former records instances of polygamy and polyandry as in the case of Droupadi. Polyandry can precede monogamy; it can never succeed it or exist in any such civilized community as the heroes of the *Mahâbhârata* are supposed to have lived in during the 'Great War' period. Polyandry, moreover, is so much opposed to the marriage laws of Hinduism that the most absurd and childish excuses are resorted to, in order to explain away the fact of the five Pândavâs having had a common wife. Such explanations can satisfy but the blind faith of a bigot. What makes the case of Droupadi still worse is that, while the wife of all the five Pându brothers, she was married only to one of them. [This is incorrect - Subba Row.] Unexplained, the case stands as one of the greatest depravity.

Again, the despondency of Arjuna on the battlefield, when he sees the hosts of human beings assembled, his own kith and kin among them, who must all be killed and slaughtered before the kingdom can be obtained, seems but natural. This consequent resolution to live the life of an exile in the jungles forever, rather than shed torrents of blood, some of it near and dear to him, for the sake of a kingdom, bespeaks of a noble, unselfish heart. Yet he is taken to task for it. That the precept of the Yoga philosophy, taught by such a personage as Krshna, an Incarnation of the great Deity Himself, should have resulted in its moving such a grand and wise hero from his high and noble resolves, and have converted him into a selfish murderer for the only purpose of aggrandizing his possessions, seems deplorable indeed. Can Yoga philosophy be made to serve a meaner or a worse purpose than this - the *Yoga* whose every aphorism breathes and inculcates self-denial? If such be the consequences of its teachings - then, away with it! And that such as been its accepted interpretation *literatim* - is evident from the very fact of Krshna being surnamed the Kucharkri (or intriguer) by the Pouraniks. After such a presentation of Krshna's character, it is no more to be wondered at, that the wise interpreters should have rejected Gautama Buddha's teachings. Indeed, it would have been a wonder had it been otherwise.

So palpably absurd is the variance between the teaching and its interpretation that many a sound scholar considers the *Gîtâ* [Some Pandits also held that *Sanatsujatîyam* and *Uttaragîta* were likewise independent philosophical discourses subsequently incorporated into the body of the Great Epic Poem. - Subba Row.] as quite a distinct work from and very injudiciously incorporated into the body of the *Mahâbhârata*. To this day, it is read and regarded by some Hindus as a record having no real connection with the Kurukshetra battle between the Pândavâs and the Kouravas; and editions accordingly compiled can be had for sale in our bazaars. [The idea of the *Gîtâ* may after all be one of the ancient books of Initiations - now most of them lost - has never occurred to them. Yet - like the Book of Job very wrongly incorporated into the Bible, since it is the allegorical and double record of (1) the Egyptian sacred mysteries in the temples, and (2) of the disembodied Soul appearing before Osiris, in the Hall of Amenthi, to be judged according to its Karma - the *Gîtâ* is a record of the ancient teachings during the mystery of Initiation. - Subba Row.]

The question now arise: Was Vyâsa Deva so short-sighted as not to have foreseen the dead-letter interpretation? Would he have so carelessly incorporated so sacred a book in so ill befitting a place of his great work, without any motive? Or was it done designedly and by some one else? As I have just shown, it seems so.

I, for one, believe that it was done after mature deliberation and that, therefore, the place and time assigned to the *Gîtâ* are both appropriate and opportune. The reasons are briefly as follows, and they are gathered from esoteric teachings. [The *Bhagavad-Gîtâ*, in its present form, *i.e., minus* the explanatory key which gave the correct interpretations to the Initiates, was incorporated after the rise of Buddhism, and when it was in the interest of the Pourâniks to conceal the great similarity of thought between Buddha's and Krshna's doctrines. Until then, the sacred writings were entirely in the hands and the safe keeping of the Initiated Brâhmana alone, and remained, therefore, unknown to the multitudes. But when Gautama Buddha - whose object was to throw open the doors of the Sanctuary to all those who were found deserving and worthy of the initiation into the Great Truths, irrespective of caste, wealth, or social position - partially revealed the secret in his public teachings; then his bitter enemies, the Brâhmana immediately after the death of the sage, destroyed and hid the key - the very kernel of the doctrine - and abandoned, to the masses, the husks. That key, contained in a work thrice as bulky as the *Mahâbhârata*, is said to have been carried away by the Buddhist Initiates into their exile; and even now the Kandy temple at Ceylon is reputed to possess a copy of it. - Subba Row.]

Although the five Pândava brothers - Yudhishthira, Bhîma, Arjuna, Nakula, and Sahadeva - are known as the sons of Pându, whence their name Pândavas, every one of them has in reality a father of his own. The *Mahâbhârata* also makes each brother the representative, or, in its peculiar phraseology, the "incarnation of his respective Father". Thus it speaks of the eldest brother Yudhishthira as the son (and also the incarnation) of Dharma. Bhima is the son (and incarnation) of Pavana. Ajuna is the son and the Avatar of Indra. Nakula and Sahadeva are the sons (and incarnations) of the

Aswini Kumârs, *i.e.,* the 'sons of the Sun'. Again, each of these personages represents some peculiar element of which he is said to be the presiding deity. Thus, 'Dharma' represents Endurance and Forgiveness, and stands for Earth; 'Pavana' is the presiding deity of the air and represents power; 'Indra', that of Âkâsha (Astral Light, Ether) which represents the soul; while the two Aswini Kumârs preside over and represent, respectively, Fire and Water, the two remaining elements. Thus we find that the five brothers or the five Pândavâs represent in reality the five elements, [In the real esoteric explanation given *only to Initiates,* the *five Pândavas* represent the *five Prânavâyus* (the five vital airs). The author of this article will do well to take up the clue and investigate all the facts given in the *Mahâbhârata* carefully. - Subba Row.] which constitute man or rather Humanity, each element being anthropomorphised into an individual. In like manner, Droupadi, their wife, though shown as the daughter King Drupada, and so named after him, is, as we find in the same *Mahâbhârata,* not Drupada's daughter at all, but another mysterious personage whose parentage is quite obscure. The fact is that, like the Pândavâs, she too is a personification; that of Yoga-Mâya or the Yoga-Illusion, and so, necessarily, is made into and becomes the common property of the five Brothers, the Elements, with their innumerable illusionary effects; while Krshna, representing the Spirit, (Paramâtma) completes the group of seven.

The summary of the above is that four of the five brothers comprise the physical or the visible gross body of man. Arjuna (the Astral Principle) is the soul and jîvâtma, the life-soul, or vital principle; and Krshna, the Spirit. The Soul and its consort Mâyâ, being always nearer to the Spirit than the rest, Arjuna, and Droupadi are represented as the bosom friends of Krshna in preference to the rest.

And now comes the question: Who the Kouravas - the foes of the Pândavâs, and especially those of Arjuna - are. Bearing in mind that those enemies are also most of them related by blood to Arjuna, we have no difficulty in pointing them out as the woes and evils to which humanity is subject, and most of which have their origin in the blood or the physical organism of man himself. The Kouravas, are therefore, no other than the evil propensities of man, his vices and their allies. The philosophy of Krshna teaches Arjuna that he must conquer these, however closely related to him they may be, before he can secure the 'Kingdom' or the mastery over SELF.

It is for this very reason that the battle-field is chosen as the scene wherein knowledge is imparted. The despondency of Arjuna is an allegory to show how often, at the very threshold of knowledge, the human soul allows its worst feelings to get the better of his reason, and that, unless he can rally round his best allies, he is lost.

The ratha (car) or war-chariot of Arjuna is being driven by the charioteer - Krshna. Ratha means, in Samskrt, the 'human body' as well as a vehicle need hardly be mentioned. In the present case it is intended to signify that should man become determined to achieve a conquest over his own passions and evil inclinations and to secure mukti or bliss to his soul, he must first listen to the whispered advices of his Spirit, whose voice is heard in the very midst of the battle that is constantly raging round him, even while the soul and the Spirit are seemingly riding in the same ratha - or body.

As a confirmation of the above interpretation, I may also remind the reader that, in their ascent to heaven, Droupadi - the Mayâ - vanishes and disappears the first, and Yudhishthira - the earth or the gross principle of the body, the last. Does not all this clearly show that there is perfect harmony between the several parts, that the whole thing has been beautifully conceived and is fully worthy of its author; that there is, in fact, no polyandry preached in it, nor any real deviation from a noble course of life toward selfish ends.

The chief difference between the Vedic and the *Gîtâ* teachings lies in the following: While the Vedâs deal with the Adwaita and Dwaita questions, *i.e.,* whether the universe or man consists of Matter and Spirit, or only of one of these two principles, [Wrong. The main point of difference between the two doctrines is this: Adwaitis hold that there is no real difference between the individual Spirit (Jîvâtma) and the Universal Spirit, (Pratyagâtma); while the Dwaitîs hold otherwise. Again, the former hold that *Spirit* alone is Sat, and everything else is Asat, or the outcome of Illusion, while the latter refuse to recognize the existence of any Illusion or Mâyâ in the Universe. - Subba Row], the *Gîtâ* clearly inculcates three in one, *i.e.,* matter, soul, and Spirit, and terms them Kshara, Akshara and Purushottama. [Not so. - Subba Row.] Hence - the temple of Jagannâth at Poori is known as the Purushottama Temple, because of its three idols - Subhadra (female), Balarâm (male), and Jagannâth or Purushottama, the sexless, Spirit, literally signifying the superior male, but *de facto*, the pure Deific Principle. This representation is also known as the 'Buddha Avatâr,' a name arising from the fact that the Buddha taught the same mystic Trinity expressed to this day in Tibet by the words: Om, Han, and Hoong, or, in Samskrt Buddha, Dharma and Sangha. The female idol has hands and feet, while the two males have neither; denoting thereby that the first or inferior man has to depend upon his gross, physical body as tools in life, while the superior man is moved to action by his soul and Spirit, and, therefore, needs no help from his physical self. So holy is that famous temple that, within its precincts, all distinction of caste disappears, and every pariah and outcaste becomes equal to the highest Brâhmana. But the discipline in it is very rigorous; no animal food or spirituous drinks being permitted to cross its threshold under any condition.

The occasion of the celebrated Car Festival is the period when pilgrims from all parts of India thickly crowd the place. The popular saying "He, who can catch a glimpse of the dwarf (meaning Jagannâth) on the car, will have no more re-births" brings, on that day, hundreds of thousands of worshipers. I have already stated above that this car is but an allegory, meaning, in reality, the human body. The true significance of the verse, therefore, is that he who can see or find the Spirit (Jagannâth, or the dwarf) enthroned in his body will have no more re-births, since he may be sure then of finding himself emancipated from sin. [Those, who have denounced for over two centuries, the 'Jagannâth car' festival as a 'heathen deviltry,' an "*abomination* in the sight of the Lord" - the ignorant, but ever traducing Padris - might do worse than ponder over this explanation. - Subba Row.] Similarly, from a crude and fanatical notion that one who gets crushed under the wheels of Jagannâth's car is saved, men had been, from time to time, throwing themselves under the sacred vehicle. The blame for so many lives lost must be laid at the door of the Brâhmanas, who, from selfish motives, had thrown away the key to the *esoteric* meaning of the sacred allegory; the real signification being that while the Spirit, Jagannâth, is driving in the car or body, if once can crush and destroy his animal soul or ego and so assimilate his spiritual Ego to the Spirit or seventh principle, he is saved.

THE BHAGAVAD-GITA

by C. Jinarajadasa

From the Proceedings of the Federation of European Sections of the Theosophical Society, Amsterdam 1904

(The scheme of transliterating Sanskrit words adopted in this essay is mainly that agreed upon by western scholars)

Among all the Aryan peoples of East and West the Hindus alone have produced a great national religion, Hinduism, and a great world religion, Buddhism. Intensely religious from the beginning of their existence as a nation, for thousands of years ever since they have maintained a religious and philosophical activity that no other nation has shown. No wonder then if the literature of India treating of religion and philosophy should exceed in volume that of any other race. Vedas, Brãhmanas, Upanishads, Sûtras, Purãnas, — these are the divisions according to age of the enormous mass of Hindu sacred literature.

But among all these works of different epochs and of varying size, the *Bhagavad Gîtã* holds a unique position. It consists of exactly seven hundred verses, divided into eighteen chapters; and yet this tiny volume is practically the Bible of the Hindus, for to all cultured Hindus of whatever sect or creed, its teachings on the deepest problems of heart and mind come with the divine sanction of God.

It has been translated from the Sanskrit into most of the vernaculars of India; it has been quoted for centuries in many a book; Hindu philosophers and scholars famous in history have written exhaustive commentaries upon it; and to swell the number of these commentaries, within recent times we have two new expositions of its philosophy, one by the late T. Subba Row in his

Lectures on the Bhagavad Gîtã, and the other in the *Studies in the Bhagavad Gîtã* by the *Dreamer*. But these writers look upon the book with the eye of faith, and they stand within the charmed circle of Hindu tradition; and so I have thought it might be of use to consider the book and its teachings from the more independent standpoint of a student of Theosophy.

To us who study Theosophy, our interest in the scriptures of the world lies solely in the fact that here and there in them we find fragments of the divine truths of Theosophy, in some clearly, in others dimly; and that a particular truth should or should not appear in a religion at a given epoch, or that we can trace its origin and development, has to us none but a historical importance. If therefore, in the analysis of the *Bhagavad Gîtã*, we find ourselves at variance with Hindu traditions, none of its philosophy is thereby and necessarily invalidated. Our aim should be to come as near the truth as we may, and it matters little if in that attempt we run counter to accepted beliefs.

In the analysis of the *Gîtã* we shall try to determine two things, first if we can glean any facts as to its authorship and date of composition, and secondly what are the leading doctrines in it.

First then as to its authorship. Hindu tradition attributes it to Vyãsa, the supposed author of the whole of the great Hindu epic, the *Mahãbhãrata*, in which the *Gîtã* appears as an episode. But Vyãsa means only *editor* or *compiler*, and as the one and the same Vyãsa is said to have edited not only the Vedas but also the Purãnas, which belong to an epoch some thousands of years later, Hindu tradition helps us little. Moreover an analysis of the epic shows at once by differences of style and by linguistic and other peculiarities, that it was composed at different times and by different hands; [R.G Bhandarkar *Journal of Bombay Branch R.A.S,* vol 10 p 85, cited in

Muir's *Metrical Translations from Sanskrit Writer's, Page* xxxv; A.A. Macdonell, *Sanskrit Literature,* pp 283 *et seq.* For the results of a careful analysis of the whole epic, see L. von Schroeder, *Indiens Literatur and Kultur.*] and this is corroborated by what is said in the epic itself, which points to the fact that the present *Mahābhārata* is the third and enlarged edition of the epic nucleus, after many episodes had been added. [Adi Parva, chap I]

We shall therefore probably never know the name of the author of the *Gītā*, but whoever he be, we see that he combined in himself the rare gifts of a poet, philosopher and mystic.

To determine the period in which the *Gītā* was composed, it is necessary to consider when first there appears in Hindu thought the idea of Avatāras or the human incarnations of the Deity. For Krishna is said to be the last avatāra of Vishnu, and the *Gītā* is the dialogue between Vishnu under the form of Krishna, and his friend Arjuna.

Now we have a fairly full account of the popular beliefs of the Hindu people in their books; the Buddhist books too describe these beliefs as they existed at the time of the Buddha. From an examination of these sources we find that in the sixth century B.C. no idea of avatāras has yet appeared, in the sense of the incarnations of Vishnu for the good of the world; in the Brāhmanas, sacred books that were composed for the most part not long before the rise of Buddhism, the stories of the avatāras appear as popular legends, but Vishnu is not connected with them. Moreover in all the Buddhist narratives of this period the chief god popularly worshiped is Brahmā, which is fully corroborated by the fact that in the oldest stories of the *Mahābhārata* itself, which date from about this period, Brahmā is the chief deity. Vishnu, who exists in the old Veda as one of the solar deities, is just mentioned in the Buddhist books, but as yet he has no prominent position in the popular mind.[Rhys Davids, *Buddhist India,* page 236] Krishna does not appear at all in Buddhist writings among the gods of the people. [Burnouf, *Introduction à l'histoire du Bouddhisme Indien:* page 121, second edition] Also we find mention of no less than sixty-two leading philosophical theories that were current at the time of the Buddha, [In the Brahmajāla Sutta] but nothing to show that there were then known the doctrines of divine grace and salvation by devotion that are so characteristic of Vishnu worship.

When little by little in the popular mind the avatāra idea arises, there is at first doubt as to which deity it is that so manifests himself. For instance in the Shatapatha Brāhmana we have the stories of the Fish, Tortoise and Boar avatāras; in it the fish that saves Manu at the time of the deluge is simply a fish and not a god in that form, [I. 8. I. I. This and the following reference to the Brāhmanas are cited by Macdonell in his article on Vedic Mythology, Journal of the R.A.S. 1895] whereas in the later *Mahābhārata* the fish, though not an avatāra of Vishnu, is an avatāra of Brahmā. [Vana Parva, Mārkandeya Samāsyā] In this Brāhmana the tortoise is the god Prajāpati or Brahmā. [VII. 5. 15] The boar in the Taittiriya Brāhmana is Prajāpati, [I.i. 3. 5, ff.] though the Shatapatha giving the same legend says nothing as to a divine manifestation, [XIV.i 2. 11] while the later Rāmāyana makes the boar Brahmā. [II. 110. Monier Williams, *Indian Wisdom,* page 330] The well-known story of Vishnu, who as a dwarf takes three steps, appears even in the Veda, and is found in later books ; though again curiously in the Taittiriya Samhitā the person who won the earth for the gods by stepping round it in three strides is not Vishnu, but Indra in the form of a she-jackal. [VII, ii. 4] Of course when we come to the late Purānas, all these legends appear as the avatāras of Vishnu only, though even then their number varies from nine to twenty-eight. [Barth, *Religions of India,* page171].

From these facts the natural inference has been drawn that about the sixth century B.C., though the worship of Brahmā was flourishing, the worship of Vishnu had hardly begun, and therefore that of Krishna could not yet have existed.

By the time of the third century B.C, however, we find the cult of Krishna already in existence and popular, alongside of the worship of Shiva; this we know from the description of India that has come down to us from Megasthenes, a Greek ambassador who lived in the country between 311 and 302 B.C. [*ibid.* pages 163 and168]; we further know that in the second century B. C. in the time of the grammarian Patañjali, the worship of Krishna was so popular that there were then dramatic representations of his life. [Macdonell, *op cit,* page414]

It follows therefore that it must have been during the period that intervenes between the death of the Buddha in the fifth century B.C. and the first mention of Krishna worship by Megasthenes towards the end of the fourth century B.C., that the great personality who is known by the name of Krishna must have appeared.

Such a statement contradicts the Hindu tradition which declares that Krishna died at the commencement of the Kali Yuga 5,006 years ago. Here certainly we have two statements that seem absolutely irreconcilable; and yet there is a theory, and one very attractive, that sheds some light on such a contradiction between scholarship and tradition. Krishna in the *Mahābhārata* plays a great part in the civil war that took place between the Kauravas and the Pāndavas. No one doubts that such a war did take place; and as we find some of the chiefs mentioned in quite early Sanskrit literature, it is quite likely that the leading events of the war go back to at least the tenth century B.C. [Macdonell, *op. cit.* 285] It is not therefore denied that Krishna, the astutest of politicians and councillors,, as portrayed in the epic, did live at this remote period, but it has been suggested that there were *two* Krishnas, and that the Krishna that has been deified is the later one that lived a few centuries before Christ, and that he has been confused with the earlier Krishna of the epic. [Adolf Holtzman, *Arjuna, a contribution to the reconstruction of the Mahābhārata*, p 61, cited by Muir, *op.cit* page xxiii. See also Lassen, *Indische Altherthumskunde*, vol I, page 488]

Strange as may appear this theory of two Krishnas, it certainly is one that explains many difficulties, not the least of which is the difficulty of reconciling the character of Krishna as we find him in the epic with the conception of Krishna as the Divine Man. If this theory be true, curiously enough it would seem to have a parallel in Christianity also, if the persistent Jewish tradition of the *Talmud* that Jesus lived 100 B.C. be founded on fact; for then we should have a similar confusion between two personalities, between the Christ who lived a century B.C., and some Jewish reformer who appeared a hundred years after him. [G.R.S. Mead. *Did Jesus live 100 B.C?* page 423]. Still, only the work of future scholars will show whether we may believe, with sufficient evidence, in such a theory or not.

Returning to the question of the date of the *Gītā* we see that at any rate it cannot have existed as a dialogue between Krishna and Arjuna before the fifth century B.C., there being as yet no worship of Krishna. The question could be quickly solved if Patañjali, the founder of the Yoga system of philosophy, of which so much is said in the *Gītā*, be the same Patañjali who wrote the great commentary on Panini's grammar during the second century B.C.; [Macdonell, *op.cit.* p 431.] the *Gītā*, must have been then written long after this system of philosophy had become popular. Now Hindu tradition says that Patañjali the Yoga philosopher was also the great grammarian; and in this case the *Gītā* cannot have been composed before the second century B.C.. But here again we do not know whether the two Patañjalis were not two distinct individuals fused into one by popular tradition [Weber, *Sanskrit Literature,* page 238]. Indeed Burnouf takes for granted that the philosopher lived before the time of Buddhism, [Burnouf, *Introduction,* page 188]. whence it would follow that the grammarian of the second century is another individual.

The late K. T. Telang, a Hindu scholar of much critical acumen, after a careful examination of the *Gītā*, puts its date as certainly before the second century B.C., and perhaps going back even as far as the fifth, [Sacred Books of the East, Volume 7 page18] and undoubtedly many of his arguments are striking and convincing. That the chief ideas of the book existed in the third century B.C. seems clear from evidence that comes to us independent of Brāhmanic traditions, for Nāgārjuna, the great Buddhist philosopher of the Mahāyāna school, who was born at the time of the Third Buddhist Council (242 B.C) is said to have been the pupil of a Brāhman who was much influenced by the teachings of the sage Krishna, and there seems little doubt that we are dealing here with the Krishna of the *Gītā*. [Kern, *Manual of Buddhism,* page 122 gives references on this to A. Schiefner's works on Tibetan Buddhism]

Yet on the other hand there are indications to show that there are parts of the book that are later than the second century B.C. For instance, in chapter 10 verse 33, Krishna says, "Among compounds I am the Dvandva". Now the meaning of this to an educated Hindu is perfectly clear, for of the six classes of compounded words in Sanskrit grammar the Dvandva class is recognised as the chief in grammatical value. But this doctrine of the superiority of the Dvandva over the other compounds is first enunciated by the grammarian Patañjali, who lived in the second century B.C.. [Pat. I. p 392, cited in Speijer, *Sanskrit Syntax,* page 151, note] Indeed the earlier grammarian Pānini it seems denied this superiority. Patañjali who commented on Pānini accepted it and taught it in his

Mahābhāshya. Now a good deal of time, must have elapsed after Patañjali, before the author of the *Gītā* could make Krishna say, "Among compounds I am the Dvandva", taking it for granted that his hearers would understand by it the superiority of the Dvandva over other compounds.

It will be apparent therefore from what has been said that the evidence is contradictory, showing that parts of the book cannot have been composed before the second century B.C., and that other parts probably were composed long before; and the easiest solution to this puzzling problem seems to be to admit that the *Gītā* originally existed in a smaller form which was expanded when it was embodied in the epic. Holtzmann even suggests that in the earlier epic there was a philosophical discussion before the commencement of the battle, on the immortality of the soul, but between Drona and Duryodhana, and not between Krishna and Arjuna. [Muir, *op.cit*, p xxii] The idea that the *Gītā* as we have it is the work of more than one hand would explain certain contradictions in the book, [2 IX. 29. "To me there is none hateful or dear". VII, 17. "For supremely dear am I to the wise man, and he is dear to me". Also XII, 14 — 20; XVI, 19 ; XVIII, 65.

V. 15. "The Lord receives neither the evil nor the good deed of any". IX, 24. "I am indeed the Enjoyer, as well as the Lord, of all sacrifices".

VI. 46. The devotee superior to men of knowledge. XII, 12. Concentration superior to knowledge. *Per contra*, VII, 18. The man of wisdom the highest, and IV, 38, Wisdom the supreme purifier] and many repetitions of the same idea over and over again; the second half of the last chapter, for instance, is merely a rapid summing up in other words of what has gone before.

Another striking peculiarity is that Krishna in the book speaks from two standpoints: at times in speaking of the Universal Self, he speaks, like the philosophers of the Upanishads, with a deep awe and reverence of "The Self, He, It, That, Purusha", and so on; and at other times he speaks directly in the first person as the Avatāra, the God, — "Such an one comes to Me". There is moreover, as many will have noticed, a certain inequality in the book, parts of which express a universal religion and are so lofty in their conception as to be unsurpassable; and yet there are other parts of the book, like those in chapter XVII dealing with the Gunas, that might be called almost trivial in contrast.

It seems therefore not unlikely that when the great epic was arranged in its final form, the *Gîtā* when included in it underwent some change; it was probably at this period that the book was limited to exactly seven hundred verses — most likely, as has been suggested, to prevent further additions — and divided into eighteen chapters, to fall into line with the epic, which is divided into eighteen books, in which the battle lasts eighteen days, and eighteen armies are engaged. It is noteworthy too that the number of the Purānas is eighteen.

With reference to the date of the *Gîtā*, it is but right to mention that a claim has been made that the book shows undoubted traces of Christian influence, and so must be post-Christian. This assertion once had the support of many Sanskrit scholars in the West, and there was much to be said in favour of it. We can trace in the history of Hindu thought the commencement in germ and the gradual development of all the leading doctrines of Hinduism and Buddhism. But the doctrine of the *Gîtā* of grace and salvation by devotion, appears in the Hindu mind fully developed and without a precursor, with startling suddenness. Worship, reverence, and fear of the Gods exist in the oldest Hinduism, and Shraddhā, faith or trust in a god, we find personified as a goddess even as early as the Rig Veda, [X. 151] and strange as it may seem it exists in Buddhism too; [*Sutta Nipāta* verses 76, 181, 183, 336, 431, 719. *Dhammapada*, vv 303, 333.] but Bhakti, love of God, is different, and appears suddenly as a new gospel and means of salvation. Wherefore scholars seeing in the *Gītā* the many sayings of Krishna that so resemble verses in the New Testament, have claimed that the leading ideas of the *Gītā* are of non-Hindu origin and have been taken from Christianity.

But in the words of Max Müller: "It is strange that these scholars should not see that what is natural in one country is natural in another also. If fear, worship and reverence of the Supreme Clod could become devotion and love with Semite people, why not in India also ? "[*Natural Religion,* Gifford Lectures, 1888, p 97] Barth, too, rejects the theory of borrowing, and says, "The book is Indian and Indian throughout. [Muir, *op. cit.*p xIi] Such learned Sanskrit scholars as Muir, [*ibid*, p xv *et seq.*] Monier Williams, [*Indian Wisdom*, pp 153, 154] and Cowell [*The Aphorisms of Shāndilya,* page viii] also see no reason why Hindu thought alone could not originate the new teachings; and even Weber, who desired so strongly to see Christian influence in the *Gītā* had to admit that it could not be proved; [*Sanskrit Literature,* p 238] and therefore we may be certain that the *Gītā* owes nothing to Christianity. In fact, again in the words of Max Müller, "Still, even if, chronologically, Christian influences were possible at the time when the poem was finished, there is no necessity for admitting them. I do not wonder at readers, unaccustomed to Oriental literature, being startled when they read in the *Bhagavad Gītā* IX. 29, 'They who worship me with devotion or love, they are in me, and I in them.' Such coincidences between the thoughts of the New Testament and the thoughts of Eastern sages will meet us again and again, because nature is after all the same in all countries and at all times."[*op. cit* pages 99-100]

Perhaps indeed a seemingly stronger case for Buddhist influence on the *Gītā* could be made out, were one so minded for many a verse of the *Gītā* seems very reminiscent of verses in the *Sutta Nipāta* and the *Dhammapada*, [Remarkable is the occurrence of the term ' *Kshetrajina* (Pāli, Khettajina), "the *Conqueror* of the Field", in *Sutta Nipāta*, Sabhiya Sutta, vv. 14, 15. Certain Brāhmans come to the Buddha and ask him to *define* it. It must therefore have been a well-recognized term of philosophy In the *Gītā*, chap. XIII we have Kshetrajña, " the *Knower* of the Field ".

Of many verses in the *Sutta Nipāta* and the *Dhammapada* the following from the latter will serve for comparison.

"Let no one forget his duty for the sake of another's, however great; let a man, after he has discovered his own duty, be always attentive to his duty". v. 166. cp. *Gītā*, III. 35.

"Self is the lord of self, who else should be the lord ? With self subdued a man finds a lord such as few can find". v. 160.

"Rouse thyself by thyself, examine thyself by thyself; thus self-protected and attentive wilt thou live happily, O Bhikkhu." v. 379.

"For self is the lord of self, self is the refuge of the self; therefore curb thyself as the merchant curbs a noble horse". v. 380 cp. *Gītā*, VI. 5, 6. and these two Buddhist works on morality, and especially the former with its archaisms in language, are undoubtedly earlier than the *Gītā*. But in reality such an attempt would not show more than that Indian philosophers, reasoning as they do on lines very similar, have certain expressions and modes of thought and similes that arise in the mind of each, without there being any borrowing one from another.

From the foregoing remarks it will be seen that we may put the composition of the *Gîtâ* as we have it now at about the first century B.C.. The evidence, it is true, is neither definite nor satisfactory; but the general tendency now-a-days is to put back the date of old Sanskrit writings, and we shall not be far wrong in claiming for the *Gîtâ* an antiquity that dates from before the commencement of the Christian era.

Moreover, the Buddha declares that in a certain manner he teaches the value of action, though he also teaches at the same time the value of non-action. (Kern, *Manual of Buddhism*, p. 71, gives the references in the Suttas). cp. *Gîtâ* IV 16, 17. The question as to the value of action, good or bad, seems to have been frequently discussed at the time of the Buddha, and in the Samaññaphala Sutta (trans, by Rhys Davids, *Dialogues of the Buddha*), we have the opinions of the then six chief philosophers.

Here we must leave the further examination of this question hoping that future scholarship may be able to settle the matter more definitely, and explain the peculiar phenomenon of the sudden appearance in India and Palestine of ideas so remarkably similar.

In dealing with the *Gîtâ* as a book of philosophy, there are certain elements in the book that are of special interest to us all as students of Theosophy. Everyone who reads the book with some attention will have noticed how often the author insists that certain systems of Hindu philosophy, the Sãnkhya and the Yoga, do not contradict each other. "Children, not the wise, speak of Sankhya and Yoga as distinct. He who is rightly devoted to even one obtains the fruits of both. That State which is reached by Sãnkhyas is reached by Yogis also. He sees [rightly], who sees Sãnkhya and Yoga as one".

(V. 4, 5). In other places also much emphasis is laid on the harmony that exists between the doctrines of these two systems.

Now though many writers have pointed out the eminently psychological and mystical character of the book, no one, as far as I am aware, has laid adequate stress on the fact that the *Gîtã* is an attempt to harmonise such important philosophical systems as existed in its day, and that it tries to find the common basis of them all. Had the book no other intrinsic merits, this peculiarly Theosophic standpoint alone would make it worthy of study by students of Theosophy. The doctrines of the *Gîtã* are very largely eclectic, and the great influence it has had in India for nearly two thousand years is due just to this eclecticism. The *Gîtã*, must surely be the earliest instance in history of the study of religion and philosophy with the aim of finding the unity underlying them all. But how this truly Theosophic task was accomplished will only be clear after an examination of what were the leading philosophical theories that the *Gîtã* tries to harmonize.

When the *Gîtã* was composed, three important philosophies were much studied. There was the idealistic philosophy of the Upanishads, which later becomes crystallised into the Vedãnta system, and this may be said to be the groundwork of the book. There were also the Sãnkhya and the Yoga systems. The author of the *Gîtã* blends all these three, pointing out their harmony with the help of the new idea of Bhakti or loving devotion. It will be necessary therefore to consider, even though hastily, the chief doctrines of these three systems, to understand the Theosophic character of the book.

It would perhaps be wrong to talk of the Upanishads as if they were the exponents of a definite scheme of philosophy, for they contain only the speculations and theories of earnest philosophers, and often the ideas of one contradict those of another; far rather should we regard them, as Max Müller has justly said, as "guesses at truth, frequently contradicting each other, yet all tending in one direction".[Hibbert Lecturer, 1878, page 317]

Nevertheless they contain ideas common to all. By careful reasoning all come to the conclusion that all nature is the manifestation of the one intelligence called Brahman; that man's Individual Soul, the Jîvâtman, is in reality the Supreme Soul, the Paramâtman, and that man's separated existence is temporary and lasting only till he shall rise above his limitations. Sometimes this Jîvâtman was the prâna, the breath; or something more subtle than the air, the ether being the âtman in nature. Or else the âtman was a small being, a homunculus, a purusha, which had its seat in the heart, where it was felt stirring, and from which it directed the animal spirits. Here it sat at its ease, for it was not larger than the thumb. It could even make itself still smaller, for it was felt making its way along the arteries, and could be distinctly seen in the small image, the pupil, which is reflected in the centre of the eye. A purusha, quite similar, appeared with dazzling effect in the orb of the sun, the heart and eye of the world. That was the âtman of nature, or rather it was the same âtman which manifested itself in the heart of man and the sun; an invisible opening at the top of the skull affording a passage for it to go from one dwelling place to another. "[Barth, *op, cit*, p 72]

Nor is there in the Upanishads any definite theory as to the first cause of manifestation. Some declare that the primordial being, Prajâpati, tired of his solitude, willed to manifest, and separating himself into male and female produced all that exists. Others hold that the primordial being himself proceeds from a material substratum, and then he is Hiranyagarbha, the *Golden Embryo*, or Nârâyana, " whose abode is the deep ". Another theory is that the primary matter extricates itself from chaos, and by its own energies becomes the cosmos, the asat becomes the sat, [*ibid.* p 69] without the direction or interposition of a personal agent.

In some of the Upanishads we get a foreshadowing of the theory of Māyā, which makes all manifestation an illusion, the one reality being [Page 20] Brahman, who never changes. This idea gets developed little by little, and later in the Vedānta system as formulated by Shañkarāchārya, it becomes the prominent feature of the modern Vedānta.

Generally in the Upanishads the first cause, the Absolute, is called Brahman, or by the pronoun That, and sometimes Īshvara, the Lord, the material cause, who however is not looked upon as a *personal* god; and the sages do not depart from this abstract notion of the first cause. In a late Upanishad, however, the Shvetāshvatara, we find it personified as Rûdra, and with its expressions of love and devotion and awe as to a "personal god" — an idea quite foreign to the older philosophers.

The Sāñkhya system, whose author is Kapila, on the other hand, is remarkable for the fact that it practically ignores the conception of Deity. It attributes all manifestation to material causes, and may be called atheistic in that there is no need in its scheme for a supreme divine intelligence. It is true that to avoid the charge of atheism some of its adherents do admit an Īshvara, a theoretical Supreme Soul, " a personified Sum of existence", but Kapila declares that the existence of Īshvara is not proved. [Aphorisms 92 and foll. Monier Williams, *op.cit* p 97] According to the Sāñkhya, Purusha and Prakriti, Soul and Matter, exist eternally. Prakriti by its own inherent energies and by modifications of its three Gunas or ingredients, produces all manifestation; Purusha, the soul, producing nothing and never changing, merely contemplates these manifestations, giving itself up to an apparent but not real union with Prakriti to realize individual existence, to experience the pleasures and disgusts due to Prakriti; weary of this, the soul presently realizes that it is radically distinct from Prakriti and so regains its original liberty. All individual souls are eternal and intrinsically equal, and each retains its individuality, remaining unchanged throughout its long experiences during many lives. The modifications of matter with which these souls temporarily unite vary greatly, and hence there are beings at different levels of intelligence.

The three Gunas are not *qualities* of Prakriti (as in the Vedānta), but actual substances that make up Prakriti. From Prakriti as the original producer, seven other producers are evolved, Buddhi, Ahañkāra and the five Tanmātras; from the Tanmātras come the five gross elements, ākāsha, air, fire, water, earth, which are productions only; and Ahañkāra produces the five organs of sense, the internal organ of the mind, and the five organs of action. Purusha, eternal and unalterable, is neither produced, nor is it productive of anything.

Coming to the Yoga system, whose founder is Patañjali, we find that it admits the Sāñkhya scheme of cosmogenesis, but differs in that it is not atheistic, and does admit God. According to the Yoga, "God, Īshvara, the supreme ruler, is a soul or spirit distinct from other souls; unaffected by the ills with which they are beset; unconcerned with good or bad deeds or their consequences, or with fancies or passing thoughts. In him is the utmost omniscience. He is the instructor of the earliest beings that have a beginning; himself infinite, unlimited by time".[Colebrooke, *Essays on the Religion and Philosophy of the Hindus,* Sāñkhya, page 159]

Such in brief is a bare outline of the philosophical systems of the Upanishads, of the Sāñkhya and of the Yoga. Now let us see what each had to say as to the realisation of the *summum bonum*.

As has been pointed out, all three systems are agreed as to what is the ultimate aim. It is to arrive at that supreme state of consciousness or existence, where the notion of individuality is merged in the realisation of the true nature of the Self. Now as long as the individual soul does not realise its real nature, it exists in the world of non-reality, and hence must submit itself to the working of the law of Karma, which measures out pleasure or pain as the result of action. After the death of the body the soul may spend millions of years in the worlds of bliss, like the gods, for good works done, or an equally long period in worlds of pain, for sins committed; but as soon as the Karma, good or bad, is exhausted, the soul is born again on earth and once more is bound upon the wheel of birth and death, with the inevitable concomitants of pleasure and pain. Obviously then, one thing and one thing only prevents the soul from arriving at the goal. It is Karma, the inexorable law of cause and effect.

For every thought, every act, sets in motion forces that must work themselves out on their generator, for good or for evil, and so long as man creates Karma, there cannot be liberation. But is it possible to escape this law? Yes, says Hindu philosophy, and by so doing only will there be salvation. And to reach this goal the Upanishads lay down many qualifications. Knowledge is the chief of them; but there must be restraint of desires: " When all desires that linger in his heart are driven forth, then mortal immortal becomes, here Brahman he verily wins. When every knot of heart is unloosened, then mortal immortal becomes. So far is the teaching".[*Katha Upanishad,* (Mead and Chatterji's translation) II, vi 15] Purity of life, restraint of the senses, and a calm mind are also necessary. "Not one who hath not ceased from evil doing, nor one with senses uncontrolled, not one whose mind is uncollected, nor one whose mind is not at peace, can gain that self by knowledge merely". [*ibid.* II, ii. 24] Profound meditation too must be practised, and it is said that " the wise should sink sense into mind; this sink in reason, sink in the Great Self reason, this in the Peace Self sink."[*ibid*, I. iii. 13] But at the same time the duties to wife and child and friend must be carefully performed, and the sacrifices to the gods must be carried out, as ordained by the scriptures. [*Taittiriya Upanishad*, I. 9].

Thus in the Upanishads in general, the qualifications are many. "Truth only — says Rāthîtar, who speaks the Truth himself. Ascetic practices — says Paurushishti, who ever lives himself this life. Study and teaching, verily — Nāka Maudgalya says," [*ibid*. I. 9] but no one definite path is outlined as the one and the only.

The Sāñkhya emphasized one side of this teaching. Not admitting a supreme divine intelligence, it does not teach man to strive for union with God; it declares that a man has but to realise that he is *not* the material world with all its fantasies evoked by Prakriti, and the goal is then reached. To do this a man must understand by careful analysis according to the Sāññkhya method of investigation, how manifestation arises. He must also renounce action, dedicating himself with all his mental faculties to cognise what is the real and what the non-real. The way of Knowledge, says the Sāñkhya, is the only way to salvation.

The Yoga system emphasised the other side of the same general teaching of the Upanishads. As was pointed out, it does admit a divine eternal consciousness; and hence it declares with the Upanishads that man must strive for union with that Īshvara. But the Yoga does not insist on knowledge, as does the Sāñkhya, but on contemplation, and then it prescribes that this contemplation is to be practised according to a special method, necessitating regulation and suppression of breath, states of ecstasy, and special postures of the body and the development of abnormal faculties. The way of ecstatic Contemplation, says the Yoga, is

These then were the paths pointed out by the Hindu philosophies before the time of the *Gītā*; and now we shall be able to see clearly how the *Gītā* unites them all, and, in the light of the new doctrine of Bhakti, loving devotion to God, shows them as not different paths but one path. For the *Gītā*, points out a new way in which man can step outside the working of the law of Karma; and in this path are two stages. Do every act, says Krishna, without thought of reward, here or hereafter, and liberation will ensue; or better still, do each act as an offering to God, and salvation is sure. Knowledge alone will not suffice by itself; it must be sought for with Bhakti, love of God. Renunciation is a means, but only if the actions are renounced as an offering to the Deity. Ecstatic contemplation and ascetic practices are useful to carry a man towards the goal, but he must have knowledge too. No duty must be renounced, but the weariness of action will disappear if each act is made a sacrifice. Pursuit of knowledge of divine things, ecstasy, all the virtues imaginable, strict fulfilment of duties, are all necessary for a man for liberation, but above all he must feel within himself the love of God, in whose name he will live and die. And thus the *Gītā* proclaims the one and the only way to be that of Sacrifice, for Sacrifice is the only act that makes no Karma, and hence the goal.

Not only with regard to the path does the *Gītā* show the common basis of the three systems of philosophy, but the same attempt is made for other teachings also. What the Upanishads and the Sāñkhya and the Yoga say as to the relation between the Individual Soul and the Universal Soul, and what their theories are as to the origin of manifestation, have already been mentioned; and on examination it will be seen that the views of the *Gītā* on the same subjects have a good deal in common with all the three systems; and, as was pointed out, it is just this fact that makes the *Gītā* so interesting to the student of religions.

Equally noteworthy is the attitude of the *Gîtâ* to the Hindu scriptures, the Vedas, which were looked upon as direct revelations from the Deity. It is quite true that long before the *Gîtâ* was written there were Hindu philosophers bold enough to declare that the Vedas were "a tissue of nonsense", [Yãska's *Nirukta,* I, 15, 16, Barth, *op.cit.* page 85], and the attitude of the early Buddhists in denying any authority at all to the Veda was only an expression of this same sentiment that rebels against orthodoxy. With these the *Gîtâ* agrees, and rejecting the *flowery speech* of those that hold that the Vedas are sufficient for all purposes (II. 42), declares that for an *enlightened Brãhman* there is as little need to go to the sacred scriptures for the knowledge he seeks, as for a man to go to a tank for water when there is water on all sides (II. 46); and yet, in a spirit of conciliation, the *Gîtâ* says that these same Shãstras are to be the authority in deciding what ought or ought not to be done. (XVI. 24.)

But all these and many other interesting questions can hardly be discussed within the limits of a paper like this; and the subject must be left here, with the hope that some student will be sufficiently interested to follow out the line of study suggested.

Before concluding this essay, there remains only to consider the teachings of the *Gîtâ* in the light of Theosophy. A student of Theosophy naturally cannot look upon the scripture of any religion from the standpoint of a sectarian, nor can he help contrasting its teachings with what he finds in Theosophy. If therefore any comments are made on the teachings of the *Gîtâ*, it is not done in a spirit of criticism; but it is because the fuller comprehension we now have of Theosophy shows all the more clearly in contrast that there is that in Theosophy not found in any Oriental religion or philosophy.

And the great difference would seem to lie in this, that we find in Theosophy a far nobler ideal of the spiritual life than what we see in either Hinduism or Buddhism. For in those religions the chief theme is always that man has but one supreme duty, which is to save his own soul. All their moral teaching, the efforts of heart and mind that they prescribe, are bent towards this same end.

One who approaches these religions after a study of Theosophy listens in vain to hear that note of universal sympathy and brotherhood that rings throughout the teachings of the profoundest of books that speak of the spiritual life, *Light on the Path*. Undoubtedly much stress is laid in the *Gîtâ* on the thought that we must see the One Life underlying all forms, and that we must look equally upon a saint, a lump of earth, or stone, or gold; but this is hardly the conception of Brotherhood that is the key-note of Theosophy. Hinduism indeed does proclaim man's divine nature, and Buddhism that there is liberty for all men; but in both there lacks the further truth that no man can attain to liberation by attending to himself alone.

Over and over again the *Gîtâ* insists that we must strictly fulfil every duty into which we are born, but it also warns us not to undertake any new duties lest salvation be delayed thereby. How different is this from what *Light on the Path* teaches: "Remember that the sin and the shame of the world are your sin and shame; for you are a part of it, your Karma is inextricably woven with the great Karma . . . try to lift a little the heavy Karma of the world: give your aid to the few strong hands that hold back the powers of darkness from obtaining complete victory".

In other ways also does the Theosophical ideal differ from that which we see in the *Gîtâ*. In the fundamental idea of the evolution of the soul, and that " its future is the future of a thing whose growth and splendor has no limit", we find in Theosophy a new hope for man that lightens a little the gloom of the misery and the pain of humanity. For though much of Hindu philosophy is profoundly true, yet the lack of just this one conception that the human soul evolves, makes one ever ask: "If the Individual Soul, divine and immutable, is identical with the Universal Soul, why then all this evolution, and the struggle and the pain that it involves ? " *That*, is all Mãyã, illusion, a dream, an unreality, says the *Gîtã*, and

'Tis nothing but a Magic Shadow-show,

Play'd in a Box whose Candle is the Sun,

Round which we Phantom Figures come and go.

[*Gîtã*, XVIII. 61:

"The Lord dwells in the hearts of all beings, O Arjuna, and by his Mãyã whirls them round, as though mounted on a machine"]

The answer is clear; but has not the answer that Theosophy gives us more of hope in it ?

Indeed one cannot but think that we who study Theosophy now see far more clearly than did many of the philosophers of old what is the real ideal to which man is destined. And that ideal is not that man should be a saint nor a wise man, nor even that his highest happiness lies in his trying to merge his own consciousness in that of Divinity. Far rather does the Divine Wisdom show us that man's aim should be to perfect himself in all ways, that he may be a worker with God, and take his share in helping the humanity of which he is a part.

With this end in view he must have the keen intellect of the sage, and the pure and gentle heart of the saint, and the devotion of the lover; and if he would be more efficacious still in his help, he must develop within himself that other side of the human soul that sees in Divinity not only Power, Wisdom and Love, but also Infinite Beauty; and it is in declaring the necessity of this many-sided development that Theosophy holds out a grander ideal for man than any religion or philosophy, in East or West, has as yet done.

Thus, though there is in Theosophy much that is not to be found in the scriptures of the world's religions, yet so lofty is the philosophy of the *Gîtã*, and so profoundly true are its teachings, that all who read the book will agree that everyone who studies and ponders over its deep philosophy must become wiser and more serene thereby; and we can therefore well; concur in what Sañjaya the seer in his enthusiastic devotion says of the book in its last verse, that " Wherever is Krishna, Lord of Devotion, and Pãrtha the Archer, there in my opinion are fortune, victory, prosperity and eternal justice".

www.ingramcontent.com/pod-product-compliance
Lightning Source LLC
LaVergne TN
LVHW041501070426
835507LV00009B/738